]

MW01093958

BUT

WHAT DOES GOD SAY?

A 25-minute Guide to a Successful Relational Future

Dr. Tommy W. Steele

NOTICE

Scriptures noted (KJV) are taken from the King James Version of the Bible.

Copyright © Dr. Tommy W. Steele,

2018 ISBN: 9781979691642

Table of Contents

He Say, She Say, but what did God Say?

"My people are destroyed for a lack of knowledge."
Hosea 4:6

This book is written to give the divine revelation of the heart of God when it comes to His thoughts and His kingdom assignment for kingdom families. What do I mean by kingdom families? Our God is a King; he has a kingdom, and those of us who are saved, or have a relationship with Him through His son Jesus Christ, are his servants. The Bible is the constitution, or spiritual laws, which comes from our King on how things are supposed to be.

Isaiah 55:8-9

"His ways and his thoughts are so much higher than ours."

Psalms 100:3

"It is he that made us and not we ourselves."

God is the manufacturer of his people and the manufacturer of all relationships; what He says about how you, as his product, are supposed to function is law because He wrote the manual.

Ephesians 2:8

"You are saved by grace through faith."

Ephesians 2:10

"For we are his workmanship (product)."

A car has to have gas, oil, and water to function, and if the gas, oil or water is not placed where it was designed, by the manufacturer, it will cause that car to malfunction. If your home is not functioning right, something is out of place. You will find principles in this book that will overhaul your family, and restore your relationships, to a place that you have always dreamed.

In America, the divorce rate has risen from 67% to 70%. That equates to 2 out of every three marriages ending in divorce. Marriage is laborious, and chances of divorce are much higher for the second and third marriages. There is a 73% chance that your second marriage will end in divorce and a 76% chance that your third marriage will end in divorce. However, divorce is not the problem; it is ONLY a symptom of a problem.

Tomorrow is not promised. Life is entirely too short, and the time is too urgent, to remain defeated over the past. Life is too short, and the time is too urgent, to repeat mistakes that could ruin your future. We have done it our

know it doesn't work. We need

manufacturer, and the guide (GOD), to get us

back on track. We have heard enough of the

He say and the She say, it is time to see What

God has To say.

Ephesians 3:20

"God is able to do exceeding abundantly above
anything you would even ask or think."

John 10:10

"The thief (Satan) came to steal, kill, and destroy; I
am come that you might have life and have it more
abundantly."

I travel around the country speaking. I

talk to many people from all walks of life.

There is one commonality in the conversations. It is our family. Often, someone asks me what it is that Satan is using to destroy and tear our

families apart. Given the opportunity to speak to every family in the world I would advise the top three ways Satan destroys our relationships are communication, sex, and finances.

This is the truth; just as improperly placing the water, oil, and gas in a vehicle causes it to malfunction, so will the misuse of communication, sex and finances tear apart your family.

Colossians 1:17

"He (Christ) is before all things, by him all things consist (or hold together.)"

I want you to listen. Any relationship that's going to make it cannot survive without

Christ. Christ is your Water. The Holy Ghost is your Oil. The Word of God is your Gas. The reason it is imperative to have Christ in your life

is not only because Jesus is a savior, but because Jesus is also a restrainer.

How many times have you been upset, and to the point that you started to take action on your own, but Jesus held you? How many times have you started to get revenge on someone for wrongdoing? In the midst of the madness, He began to speak to you and reminded you, "Vengeance is mine; I will repay," "Recompense no man evil for evil," and "Don't let evil take you over, but you overcome evil by doing that which is good."(Romans 12:17-21) God said in essence, this is not your battle, but the battle is mine. God will fight the battles for us, but we need the guide.

First Lady Steele and I have been married for 39 years. I give God all of the glory. We both came out of single-parent homes and never had an example to tell, or show, us how to have a

family the way God designed it. You look at us now, and it is a far cry from when we first met. You will hear me call her sweet, while she calls me honey. I don't blame my father and mother nor do I blame her father and mother. They could only give us what they had, that's why I am so thrilled to share these principles. I know if it had not been for the Lord on our side we wouldn't have survived over the years. I don't know where we would be and I give him all the glory for keeping my family together.

Psalms 107:20

"He sent his word, and healed them..."

I will never forget the day my wife came to me and voiced that she was not happy in the relationship. We had only been married for two years. I had no idea what to do. I had only been saved for about two years and had no idea what to tell her. I only had an idea. I said to her, "Baby I am not happy either. Let's give it 30 days to work, and this is what I will do. I'm going to read the bible and find out what God said about me being a man, and I want you to read it to find out what God said about you being a woman. If after 30 days it doesn't work you can go your way, and I will go my way.

To God be the glory that 30 days has turned into 39 years. Always remember anything long and lasting begins and ends with God. Now I am going to share with you the principles God has used to keep First Lady and me together all these years. Outside of Jesus, she is the most significant friend I have.

Principle I:
Communication

We have learned how to communicate, and it has been very impactful in keeping my marriage healthy.

Ephesians 4:29

"Let no corrupt communication come out of your mouth, but that which is used to edify…"

In other words, what comes out my mouth and what comes out of the mouth of my wife should be used to build each other up. Our words should never be used to tear each other down. There are thousands of people who cannot communicate with their spouse. It would blow your mind to know the actual number, but it explains why the divorce rate is so high.

There are many more people who cannot communicate with their children, coworkers or brothers and sisters in Christ. We have done precisely what The Enemy wanted us to do; we have allowed him to drive a wall between us, and others, to keep the door open for him.

Ephesians 4:27

"Neither give place to the devil."

This translates to don't let him put his foot in the door. Once his foot in the door he is coming in your house, and maybe he is already there. I believe by the time you finish reading these principles he will have to pack his bag and get out.

How was he able to enter? Do you remember when your mate, or even your children, came and told you something that you perceived as negative, or when they said something you disagreed with? Your response allowed entrance. You began to say something like this, "You are stupid, and that's the dumbest thing I have ever seen!" Then you began to call them names and say things like, "You idiot. If I put your brain in a bird, it would fly backward, and you can't do anything right with your sorry self."

Proverbs 18:21

"Life and death are in the power of your tongue."

You can speak life into your family, or you can destroy your family, but what comes out of your mouth will either uplift them or destroy them. It will either build them or break them. After the screaming and hollering at each other has stopped, the walls have gone up, The Enemy is in, and nobody is willing to talk about anything. We have lost our foundation in communication. Instead, we are now the great pretenders. We go on pretending that everything is alright because we cannot deal with the real issues. Each talk leads to drama, and it becomes easier to ignore it. And then we hear comments such as, "I'm not talking to them, I'm not going through all that drama."

Never forget Ephesians 6:10-12 tells us that Satan has assigned his Devils to all of us.

Just as the military has different orders of command, Satan has, according to Ephesians

6:12, principalities, powers, rulers of darkness, and spiritual wickedness in high places. These satanic arsenals which he has assigned to you and me.

Every day Satan has a meeting with his satanic arsenal to discuss how to destroy our families. He is like the lions you see on the geographical shows, once they set their sight on something they don't stop until they capture their prey.

1 Peter 5:8

"Be Sober(alert), be vigilant(watchful), because our adversary the devil walk about as a roaring lion seeking whom he may devour."

We provide the ammo. Notice in Ephesians 2:2, he is called the prince and the power of the air. His destiny is hell, but his domain is the atmosphere. He listens to our conversations, then he takes it and uses it as a weapon against us. For example, when he hears you say you can't talk to your mate, or hears your children say they can't talk to you, he will find someone for them they feel comfortable talking to.

Listen to me real close; you must always be aware of the enemy. He has a woman for the man, a man for the woman, and trouble, or mislead teens, for your sons and daughters. It always starts innocent but ends up destructive. Let me explain what I mean. Isaiah 3:9 says, *"Your countenance will witness (or tell on you)."*

In the workplace, most men work around women, and typically all women work around men. During the day our children are around other misguided, mislead children.

When you go to work, or school, and you are discouraged or depressed, your peers will ask you what is wrong. Most of the time, it is a woman asking the man, a man asking the woman, and a misguided teenager asking your child. If you respond "Nothing" then they reply, "Come on now as long as I been around you something is wrong," and that is when you open up. You begin to express the woes of your spouse, or parents., as they listen intently and make you feel valued.

At the onset, you all are just friends. You have no intentions of doing anything wrong, but you discover as you talk to them that they are not beating you up with words; that they encourage you, the respect you, they show affection toward you and remind you that things will be okay. They are like cold water to a thirsty soul. You cannot wait until the next day to get back to talk to them, and before you know it, your emotions began to lean toward that man, that women or that classmate because they make you feel worth something. Many affairs start this way. Before you know it, that man is leaving his wife, that wife is leaving her husband, and that teenager is out of control.

This lends itself to a broken-hearted family. If we know that verbally assaulting each other will divide and separate us while encouraging one another will bring us together, why don't we treat each other better and keep our homes happy?

Crying over your pass won't fix your future. I'm not underestimating anyone's pain. I have pain. We all experience anguish and pang in different ways, and some of us feel hurt worse than others. In spite of all that you have been through and all that you are going through, regardless of what people have said about you and done to you, God still has you here to let you know they cannot define who you.

Psalms 139:14

"I am fearfully and wonderfully made."

You don't need anybody to make you somebody. When God created you, you were already somebody. He let you meet Jesus, not to show you are a nobody, but that you are a somebody. You have allowed yourself to be a victim instead of a victor long enough. If God were done with you, you would not be here. Lift your eyes to the hills from which cometh your help, your help cometh from the Lord!

No more he say, she say, let's find out what God has to say! What I have discovered is most men don't understand women, and most women don't understand men. I am not an expert, but God has brought the First Lady and

I a long way from where we used to be. Allow me to share with you what I have learned about a woman.

The Woman

In 1 Peter 3:7, I am told by God to dwell with them according to knowledge. This reinforces what the Lord said in the beginning that "my people are being destroyed for lack of knowledge." A woman is the most spectacular creature God has ever placed on this planet. A woman is intelligent, creative and full of wisdom. Just as a car has to have gas, oil, and water in the right place to function properly, she has to have the needs of her life met to operate flawlessly. Now, what doe women need to function?

First and foremost a woman needs love. Ephesians 5:25 tells the Husbands, "Love your wives, even as Christ also loved the church, and gave himself for it." How did Christ love the church? Christ loved the church sacrificially and unconditionally.

John 3:16

"For God so loved the world, that he gave his only begotten Son, that whosoever believeth in him should not perish, but have everlasting life."

He loved the world so much that he gave himself and became God's sacrifice for us. In other words, a wife she should never have to fight to be first place in her husband life. He should give her first position, above his family, friends, co-workers, and constituents. The only person that should have the first place above her is her Lord and Savior Jesus Christ.

When friends, or family, come along and suggest going out, but your wife says, "Baby I wanted you to roll with me," her wishes ought to take president over everybody else. We should not only love our wives sacrificially, but we should love our wives unconditionally. Our Lord has never said I love you if you do this or if you don't do that. His love for us is unconditional! Our love for our wives should not waver. Consider the times we have made mistakes, and our Lord keeps right on loving us, forgiving us and forgetting what we have done.

Jeremiah 31:3

"..Yea, I have loved thee with an everlasting love..."

In other words don't use houses, cars, money, sex, or anything as a condition of love.

Most men don't realize their wife does appreciate the material items, but the most notable thing you can give her is you. A lot of men think just because they give her stuff she ought to be satisfied. Always remember, nothing can take the place of you, and that's why she complains! She might say, "You don't ever spend any time with me," all the while riding around in a brand new Lexus, but that is because material things don't replace you. Ephesians 5:25 says, "Christ loved the Church, and Gave (Himself) for it." He did not just say I love you; he gave himself to prove it.

Secondly, she needs a conversational partner. Most men don't understand that a woman is an incubator. What is an incubator you might ask? It is a container designed to make things grow. Because of her ability to give life, she will take whatever you give her, multiply it and give it back to you. Let me explain. If you give a woman a word, she will give you in return a sentence. If you give a woman a sentence, she will give you in return a book. If you give a woman your seed, she will give you in return a baby. If you give a woman food, she will give you in return a meal.

Most men say I don't know how to have a conversation on a continual basis and I don't do a lot of talking. I have been in restaurants, with my wife, and seen couples sitting together. I watched their interactions, and the only time they spoke was to order their food. There was a particular instance when my wife and I were in a fish camp eating. I noticed a man and his wife were sitting there together. The man read a newspaper the entire time and never said a word to his spouse.

All you have to do to have a conversation with a woman is to ask her how her day was and she will take it from there. Men, you have to get in her world. Know her shoe size, dress size, her favorite color, her favorite dessert, her hobby, her dreams and her pain. Know what makes her tick, but know what lights her up. This way we realize how to dwell with them according to knowledge.

Sometimes, the enemy will make you think the grass is greener somewhere else when all you have to do is water your garden. How many times have you seen a man let a woman go, or a woman release her man? Soon after, you see them with their new partner, and you think, "I don't see what he wants with her" or "What does she want with him?" But, they are different from the man, or woman, you saw in their last relationship. They were not like that before. It is not so much that they have changed. All they needed was watering the way God said, not the way he said, or she said.

Thirdly, a woman needs affection, and without it, she cannot function right. What is affection? It is holding her hand, telling her how pretty she is, telling her what she means to you, telling her how good she looks, taking her out to dinner just because, phone calls on lunch break, and random cards in the mail. Affection is holding her when she is hurting and kissing her outside of sex. It is getting the florist to send her flowers just because, no holiday or birthday required. Affection is your connection to her and your gifts of acclamation.

Principle II:

Sex

Sex is a necessary form of communication between a husband and wife. A woman has to have sex just as a man has to have sex. However, most men don't realize that sex to women is different than sex to a man.

To a man, sex is an act, but to a woman, sex is an experience.

A man is like a microwave (Ding) always ready. A woman is like a Crockpot; it takes a minute to warm her up. Sex starts in the morning with a hug and kiss before you go to work or a note on the mirror. "Roses are red; violets are blue, it's hard for me to go to work when I look at you." A phone call at lunch.

"Hey baby, I'm thinking about you." A text. "I can't wait to see you."

Sometimes you may have to set the atmosphere for your wife. Run her tub full of water, put some bubbly in it and outline the bathtub with candles. Play some soft music; light up the bedroom with her favorite scents and watch your wife pass out. (PS: don't you tell her I told you). Wash her back, and tell her what she means to you. Sometimes, men, just light the candles, put on some soft music, and talk.

However, 1 Corinthians 7:1-5, tells us that for a man to avoid fornication, we must let every man have his own wife and every woman have her own husband. Beyond Jesus, the most powerful force on this planet is sex. A man needs to have sex. But sex alone is not the issue. The issue is sex that is not directed in the way God designed it to be.

When it comes to marriage, women cannot afford to use sex as a weapon. Sex is already a weapon. There are not enough words to express how commanding sex is in a man's life. Only a man can fully comprehend what I am saying, and maybe it's because when God created man, he said, "be fruitful and multiply." He is carrying the seed that produces life! While a woman is a receiver, a man is a giver. He was created to reproduce. Sex is an experience to women, but sex is an act for a man. While you are waiting for him to get it right hold him tight because he has to have it, and that's not he said, or she said, that's what God said.

What happens when you go to a service station, and it says out of order? You find another service station! A wife should never shut her "service station" down. Keep it open, and with a sign that says premium octane and a flashing light that says OPEN. The devil is working overtime to get you to close up, or shut down, your station so that man can be tempted to go somewhere else.

The Bible (I Corinthians 7:5) tells us the only time we should be apart is if we are fasting and praying. He then says come together quickly, before Satan tempt you for your incontinency. Ladies always remember, you are motivated by what you hear, and a man is motivated by what he sees. Take the lock off the housecoat and look nice for him. Be his every woman! Spice it up. When he comes home after a long day, change into another woman by getting you a colored wig, fix it where he never knows what to expect by creating an element of surprise. It's not always about sex, but just keep your marriage from becoming dormant. Enjoy the experience with your spouse and remember what goes on in your bedroom is nobody else's business.

Hebrews 13:4

"Marriage is honorable, and the bed is undefiled.."

I'm just saying; we better stop worrying about he said and she said. We better start worrying about what God said. As I mentioned, a woman has to have the right gas, oil, and water to function accordingly; so does a man. A woman has to have love, a conversational partner, affection, and sex, but a man has to have different gas in his tank to function.

You cannot put the same gas you put in your tank in his tank. If you do, he will malfunction. God made us the same, but he made us different. Have you ever wonder what's wrong with your man when you give him gas. Have you considered it's the wrong kind of gas? You say, "What does a man need?" There are no ifs, ands, or buts, about what a man needs. I will tell you what I know.

The Man

The most basic, yet essential need oa man is respect, and without it, he will malfunction.

Ephesians 5:33

"Wife see that she reverence(respect) her husband."

As the most substantial need of a woman is love, the most significant need of a man is respect. Without respect, he will never be the man that he is supposed to be. Listen to the cry of street gang members when they are arrested for a crime. What is most commonly heard is, "They are not going to disrespect me." That is because this is the greatest need of a man.

Men already feel disrespected in society while on their job, and at school. The one place he should be able to come to, from the time he is a young boy until a grown man, and feel respected is in his home. He needs to be made to feel his life has value. Whenever he speaks, listen. He may not always be right, but he needs to know that his words have value, especially in his own home.

There is not a man on earth who has it all right, but at the end of it all, he needs to know his wife appreciates him. Working, and taking care of his home, while providing for his family is honorable. His wife should brag about what he is doing right while praying for what he is doing wrong. I promise you he does more right than he does wrong, but the devil will get you to focus on the wrong and forget about the right.

Tell him how proud of him you are. Remind him how much you appreciate him. Tell him how much you believe in him. You will see your man, or even your sons, rise to a level that you never witnessed. They will do everything they can to show you how much they love and appreciate you. You will be his world's greatest cheerleader and watch what happen, because you, my friend, just gave him the gas that makes his car function right.

Secondly, a man has to have a recreational partner; someone that will get in his world. Every man has some hobby, whether it be football, basketball, fishing, hunting, baseball or collecting cards. You may not like his hobby; it's not so much about the hobby as it is about you being there. It's about you spending time with your honey. (Bees like honey! Joke)

Have you noticed how excited he gets when those that are in his world come around? If you ever wonder to yourself, "Why doesn't he get excited about me as he does them?" It's because they have chosen to get in his world. If you are not careful, it will cause a spirit of jealousy to arise in your heart every time that person, place, or thing comes around. It will upset you, and you will say to your husband, "Don't they ever have other things to do?"

What you are saying is they are taking my space and my place. He may not realize it, and you may not either, but they are providing the gas that is needed to make him function right. If you want to shut down their service station and open up yours, you need to get in his world.

Something both of you need to understand: A man is a logical thinker and woman is an emotional feeler. Let me explain.

You would not believe the arguments that are started because men and women do not understand that a man is a logical thinker. My wife and I have admittedly had some. When a man is given information, he has to process it before he gives it back. Let me explain. When someone, or something, hurt a woman she will come to her husband expecting him to do something about it immediately. When, or if, he doesn't do, or say, something about it at the moment she feels like he doesn't care, so he will say or do, something just to appease her at the moment. He knows if he doesn't respond his wife will feel like he is not invested. He has to prove to her that he is devoted.

After he has had time to think about the situation he will return. He might say, "Baby, you know that conversation we had the other day..." and he will then proceed to give her the answer. In some instances, it may be contrary to what he did or spoke the week before. This could cause her to feel like he is untrustworthy and have her utter words such as, "That's why I don't believe nothing you say. One minute you are this way, the next minute you are that way. You don't know what you believe yourself." And on and on it goes. All of this because 90% of all men do not understand they are logical thinkers.

We, as men, deal with life's question from the inside. So ladies when you are upset about something, always remember just because he doesn't have the answer at the moment; it doesn't mean he doesn't care. Give him a moment to think about what you gave him. I promise he will give you answer. If you attack him, you will shut him down.

Now, on the other hand, you ladies are an emotional feeler you speak. When we speak, you start to feel, and because of this, it's easy for your feeling to get hurt. It's easy for a man to take your feeling for granted. Not understanding he is a logical thinker, and you are an emotional feeler, what most men don't understand is how easy his words/actions impact you. I am no expert, just a work in progress, with personal experience.

What I am sharing has kept my wife and me together for 39 years, to God be the glory. We found out early, it's not what he said, or she said, it's what did God said. What I have found out is as men we don't need to take your feelings for granted. When you speak, you are telling us what you feel. It's amazing how many relationships have blown up, or split up, because most women don't understand their husband, or any man, is a logical thinker. And most men don't realize that their wives, or women, are emotional feelers.

I have discovered, we don't have to have another woman or man. We need to allow God to fix us. If we don't fix us, we will repeat the same thing no matter who we get into a relationship with. I tell men all the time, and I tell ladies as well, everything you need is in your house, but your problem is he say, she say because no one wants to hear what God said.

There is another thing we need to realize as men when God created man he made him from the dust of the ground. After God made the man, he never went back to the dust again! When God made a woman, he reached inside of the man, and brought her out of the man, to teach man that everything you need is already inside of you. Your wife is you in a female body.

Ephesians 5:28-29

"For no man ever hated his own flesh, but nourished it and cherisheth it. He that loveth his wife loveth his own self."

Ladies remember in Genesis 2:18, God made you a helpmeet. Think of this way, if I hired you to work for me at Church, I did not hire you to take over; but to help me. That's what God created you to be to your husband. Be his strongest help me.

You will discover the man you were looking for; you still have him. Because most men feel like their presence in the home means nothing, the average man is not thinking about how to be closer to his family. They are thinking about ways to get out! A friend of mine ask a young lady, "Why can't I as your pastor reach your generation?" She replied, "It's very simple sir, we don't speak the same language. You cannot hear us, and we cannot hear you."

Remember, in Genesis 11:6-8, when Nimrod and a group of people were trying to build a tower to see whose top would reach into heaven and the Lord came down to see what they were doing. Once God realized what they were attempting, his response was, "The people are one, and they all speak the same language. Anything they set their heart to do they will do it."

You show me a husband and wife, along with their children, speaking the same languages. All the powers of hell cannot stop them, because it is no longer he say, she say, it is what God said. But what did God say about your finances?

Principle III:
Finances

A nother area Satan uses to tear our families apart is the area of finances.

I don't know anything that has ruined more families, caused more pain, destroyed more kingdoms, and caused more stress-related Ulcers. Nothing causes more stress and more deaths than money, yet money is not the problem.

1 Timothy 6:10

"The love of money is the root of all evil."

It's not money itself; it's the love for money and what you do with it that is causing the problem. Statistics have shown, by the time the average person reaches age 65, they will have $250.00 in their savings account. This is not the will of God for our lives.

III John 1:2

"Beloved, I wish above all things that thou mayest prosper and be in health..."

John 10:10

"Satan came that he might steal, kill, and destroy."

Well enough of the he say, she say! What did God say? You may have been born with a silver spoon in your mouth, but when I grew up, we were glad just to have a spoon. We didn't need anyone to teach us about finances because we had none.

My mother and her siblings lived with their father in a big, old house with no insulation. To live in that house, they picked cotton, clean houses, and raised all of their food. This was their pay until my mother was able to get a job in a textile mill. She worked for 42 years at this textile mill. We didn't live week to week; instead, we lived day to day. But God put us in a new day.

Matthew 6:33

"But seek ye first the kingdom of God and his righteousness, and all these things shall be added unto you."

Proverbs 4:5

"Get wisdom (discernment to use what you know), get understanding(the insight to make good Judgement)..."

The God we serve is a God of principle, and he is a God of order. I don't claim to be an expert on finances but let me give you what I have learned that will get your finances back on track.

1. Develop a mindset that everything you have belongs to God.

1 Timothy 6:7

"We brought nothing in this world, and it is certain we are taken nothing out."

It will take a lot of stress off of you when you realize that what you have is God's. If it's God's house, car, business, and family then it is not yours to maintain. Think about it; I don't worry about your car payment, or your house payment because it's not mine to worry about; you only worry about what is yours!

2. Keep good records. Have you ever ask yourself where is all my money going? You need to slow down and write down where you are spending your money. Keeping track of what goes out allows you to see what is a necessary expense versus what is not.

3. Tithe Off of everything that touches your hands.

Malachi 3:10

"Bring all the tithe into the storehouse."

Don't let anybody fool you. God's people tithed before The Law, during The Law, and after The Law. Read Genesis 14 when Abraham was returning from the slaughter of the king of Shinar. He not only defeated the king, but he brought back Lot (his Nephew), and he took all their goods. In verses 18 -20 (of the same chapter), Abraham meets Melchizedek the priest of the most high God, who was, I believe, Jesus. He gave tithes of it all. He did not give some, but all. (Read more about Melchizedek in Hebrews 7, and also in Genesis 28:22.)

Jacob told God, "All that you give me I'll surely give you a tent." This was before the law.

Leviticus 27:30

"And all the tithe of the land, whether of the seed of the land or of the fruit of the tree, is the Lord's; it is holy."

That's was under the law.

Matthew 23:23

"Woe unto you...for ye pay tithe ...and have omitted the weightier matters of the law, judgment, mercy, and faith..."

Luke 6:38

"Give, and it shall be given unto you; good measure, pressed down, and shaken together, and running over, shall men give into your bosom. For with the same measure that ye mete withal it shall be measured to you again."

Two things happen when you tithe: 1. You get divine favor, and 2. You inherit God's thoughts. Both of which are priceless!

Isaiah 55:8

"For my thoughts are not your thoughts, neither are your ways my ways."

God thoughts and ways are not like our own; they are so much higher. My grandfather used to say when I was young, "plant gardens so that your family will have something to eat." There was no need of him getting mad at the ground, or expecting something to come out of it when he never put a seed in the ground. You have to give it something so it will have something to work with.

4. Develop a Budget. In other words, find out what you have coming in and how much you have going out each month. Learn to live within your means; don't try to keep up with anybody else. I know you think you wish you had what "they" have, but if you knew their debt you would be glad to keep your own. Always remember everything has a season. It might be your neighbor's season now, but your season is coming, so dream big. If you are giving, dream big, because if you could see where God is taking you, it would blow your mind.

Habakkuk 2:2-3

"And the LORD answered me, and said, write the vision, and make it plain upon tables, that he may run that readeth it. For the vision is yet for an appointed time, but at the end, it shall speak, and not lie: though it tarry, wait for it; because it will surely come, it will not tarry."

The one thing about our God is he will keep his word.

Numbers 23:19

"God is not a man, that he should lie…"

John 14:2

"…If it were not so, I would have told you."

5. Start a savings account. I don't care if it's with $20.00, your goal should be to get to $1000 and call it an emergency fund. You will only use this fund for emergency purposes; not shopping. Think about the times you have experienced an emergency. It has cost you between $500 to $1,000 usually. Whether it's car tires, or a microwave, or something else in the house, it usually cost $1,000 or less.

Years ago I asked my mentor, a white man, "What is the difference between a black man and a white man?" He replied, "Steele, you have two problems. One, you have no inheritance." He continued, "When I got married, my father-in-law gave me 32 acres of land, where roughly 98% of all black people start out with zero." He kept going, "And secondly, social discrimination."

He and I were standing together in a parking lot with the view of a company building. He said to me, "Steele, you see that company down there?" I said, "Yes sir." He replied, "If you and I went down there and applied for a job, nine times out of 10, they would hire me because I am white." He then said, "If we do get hired, I am not going to look at your check, and you are not going to look at mine. They will pay me one wage because I am white while paying you another because you are black, and we are both doing the same job." He continued to say, "That is an example of social discrimination." When I understood this, I realized I am a trailblazer. I understand that some of the things I do must be for those in my future, which leads me to my next point.

6. Insurance. Insurance is one of the main ways you can set your family up for their future. When I was

growing up, my mother used to say, "I am not getting all that insurance." She would add, "I just need enough to get me in the ground." Now, I am not criticizing her because you can only give what you know.

II Corinthians 12:14

"...For the children ought not to lay up for the parents, but the parents for the children."

Every father and mother has to look beyond themselves and see their children, and grandchildren. I would encourage you to get as much insurance as you can afford. Start at $100,000 (if you can afford it) and move up. This way your children and grandbabies can have something to start off with, or at minimum get out of debt with. Teach your children the concept of owning a business, versus working a job. Man can take your job, but he cannot take your gift.

There is more financial security in ownership.

Proverbs 18:16

"A man's gift maketh room for him, and bringeth him before great men."

Teach your children how to handle money and to understand finances. A $20 mindset will turn 1 million dollars into a $20 bill, but a million dollar mindset will turn $20 into 1 million.

Proverbs 23:7

"For as he thinketh in his heart, so is he"

A lot of the problem with God's people is not the 10%; it is learning how to manage the 90% the way God intended.

7. Set a Goals for the next 5 years. I am going to say this again, do not try to keep up with anyone else. Live within your means, plan and pray for what you want. For example, we know every year on December 25 Christmas is coming, yet many of us wait until a week before Christmas to shop. It takes everything we have to get what we want, because we did not plan for what we knew was coming, and we start out the new year paying for the last year.

We have twelve months every year before Christmas. If you take $20 a week, that's $80 a month, and deposit it into a saving account, at Christmas you will have saved $960, and yourself a ton of stress! Anything you want and any place you want to go, plan for it! It will take a lot of financial pressure off of you, and your family. I believe our God wants the best for his children, so dream and dream big.

Special Thanks

I would like to first give thanks to my wonderful savior, The King of Glory, the Lord Jesus Christ. Without God, I would not even have a story to tell.

I would like to thank my lovely wife, Tonda Steele. She has been the support I needed to keep me going all these years, praying with me and for me. I would like to thank my family: my two sons, Michael and Joshua Steele, my precious daughter-in- law Aimy Steele, my God sent grandbabies, Michaela, Mariah, Michael Jr., Maya and Miles, and my gracious mother-in-law Hazel Blackmon. My amazing newly born grandson Ayden Joshua Steele and my special son Freddie.

Thank you for all of your love and support.

For speaking engagements contact:

New Life Baptist Church

1281 Biscayne Drive

Concord, North Carolina 28027

(704) 782-6215

www.NewLifeConcord.org

PUBLISHING

P.O. Box 264 Prosper, Texas 75078

Positioned2ProsperBooks@gmail.com